Catalogue No. 170

ENGLISH TOPOGRAPHY
in a Collection of

FINE OLD COLOURED AQUATINTS

comprising Prints in brilliant state
of

LONDON OXFORD CAMBRIDGE
VIEWS ON THE RIVER THAMES
and
AROUND THE COAST OF GREAT BRITAIN

offered by

DULAU & COMPANY, LIMITED
32 OLD BOND STREET
LONDON, W.1
Established in 1792

Telephone: *Telegrams:*   *Cables:*

1,000,000 Books

are available to read at

---

www.ForgottenBooks.com

Read online
Download PDF
Purchase in print

ISBN 978-0-266-11623-3
PIBN 10939973

This book is a reproduction of an important historical work. Forgotten Books uses
state-of-the-art technology to digitally reconstruct the work, preserving the original format
whilst repairing imperfections present in the aged copy. In rare cases, an imperfection in
the original, such as a blemish or missing page, may be replicated in our edition. We do,
however, repair the vast majority of imperfections successfully; any imperfections that
remain are intentionally left to preserve the state of such historical works.

1 MONTH OF
FREE
READING

at
www.ForgottenBooks.com

By purchasing this book you are eligible for one month membership to ForgottenBooks.com, giving you unlimited access to our entire collection of over 1,000,000 titles via our web site and mobile apps.

To claim your free month visit:
www.forgottenbooks.com/free939973

CLOVELLY ON THE COAST OF NORTH DEVON

NO. 383

NOTE

All the Prints described in this Catalogue are guaranteed to be FINE ORIGINAL IMPRESSIONS of the date stated, and as such will enter DUTY FREE into the United States of America.

In order to facilitate the sending of PAYMENT with ORDER all prints will be despatched POST FREE.

These prints make excellent Wedding Presents.

FOREWORD

"It is not unlikely that the day may arrive when the connoisseur of a future age shall pause upon an aquatinta print, with the same solemn delight, as those of our day are wont to do upon a woodcut of Albert Dürer, an etching of Hollar, or a production of any ancient engraver."—SAMUEL PROUT in 1813.

SAMUEL PROUT's prophecy has come true. There is a fashion in prints as in most things, and it is interesting to watch the emergence into popularity of some new favourite as an old one declines into obscurity. To-day the sombre mezzotint and line-engraving are relegated to the portfolio, while the colour-print is framed and occupies a place of honour on the wall. During the post-war years the demand for colour has been insistent, and in no branch of art has this been more strikingly demonstrated than in old Prints. All types of old coloured prints have been and continue to be favoured—the coloured Naval and Sporting print; the beautiful French coloured engraving; the quaint and decorative hand-coloured etchings of Birds and Flowers; the old hand-coloured engraved Map; the coloured Lithograph ; and the COLOURED AQUATINT, with which this catalogue deals. The Dictionary defines an Aquatint or Aquatinta as:

"A method of etching on copper by which a beautiful effect is produced resembling a fine drawing in sepia, biastre or Indian ink. This is performed by covering a prepared copper plate with a ground of resin coloured black by powder of asphalt. On this the design is traced, and a complicated series of operations with varnish and dilute aqua-fortis is gone through till the effect is produced."

The careful study of a fine aquatint will reveal that the process is remarkably successful in its accurate and delicate reproduction of water-colour drawings worked in simple washes, but it must be noted that the brilliant coloured aquatint is not achieved without the aid of hand-colouring. The production of the coloured aquatint, therefore, has two distinct stages (1) the engraving and printing, and (2) the colouring by hand. Usually two, but sometimes three, neutral tints were employed in the printing of the plate, a blue tint for the sky and distance, and a brown for the buildings, trees, and fore-grounds. Only the broad surfaces could be covered in this way owing to the difficulty experienced in keeping the colours within their prescribed boundaries. The delicate and varied work had perforce to be left to the final touches of the hand-colourist, whose occupation called for much skill. From the latter half of the 18th century the colouring of prints was a regular industry and in its earlier stages formed the apprentice-work of some of our great water-colour artists, including J. M. W. Turner and Thomas Girtin. It is the individual touch of the hand-colourist, heightening the already liquid and trans-lucid effect of the printed surface, which gives to the coloured aquatint its peculiar and enduring charm. A brilliant impression of a coloured aquatint crystallizes all the elusive beauties of a fine water-colour drawing, and has a delicacy, refinement, and purity not often found in any of its successors in the realm of coloured prints.

The aquatints described in this Catalogue are guaranteed to be brilliant impressions in fine state, representing some of the best work of those architectural and landscape draughtsmen and aquatint engravers who combined in so pleasant a fashion to place on record the England of a hundred and twenty-five years ago.

Fine Views of

18TH-CENTURY LONDON

Comprising all the Principal Public and Private Buildings, Places of Entertainment, Hospitals, Prisons, the Legal and Government Buildings, and some attractive prints of

THE THAMES

All the drawings for this series of coloured aquatints were made by A. Pugin and Thomas Rowlandson. Pugin was responsible for the architecture and Rowlandson for the figures. The collaboration was a very happy one, the lively groups of persons in the famous caricaturist's best manner form a most attractive addition to the careful architectural setting of Pugin.

The engraving in aquatint is by J. Bluck, J. Hill, and J. C. Stadler.

The plates measure 10⅜ in. × 8 in. printed surface, with good margins beyond this, making a total measurement of 13⅜ in. × 11 inches.

All are brilliant impressions published during the years 1808, 1809, and 1810.

7

Title of Plate.	Price.

ACADEMY, ROYAL. Somerset House
1 An interior showing students drawing from the life   £1 10 0

ACADEMY, ROYAL. Somerset House
2 An interior of the Exhibition Room during a show of paintings. A crowded scene   2 2 0

ADMIRALTY
3 Interior of the Board Room, with a meeting in progress   2 12 6

ASTLEY'S AMPHITHEATRE
4 Interior of a crowded circus, with equestrian circle and orchestra   1 10 0

ASYLUM, OR HOUSE OF REFUGE FOR FRIENDLESS GIRLS
5 The dining-hall with the quaintly dressed girls seated at long refectory tables. Established in Lambeth by Sir John Fielding in 1758   : 10 0

AUCTION ROOM AT CHRISTIE'S
6 An excellent print of the famous Room, with a Sale of Pictures in progress. Rowlandson's drawing of a varied company of buyers is particularly good   3 3 0

BANK OF ENGLAND
7 Interior of the Great Hall, with many figures   3 3 0

BARTHOLOMEW FAIR
8 The Fair at night, with a large crowd surrounding the booths, swings and roundabouts   2 2 0

8

Title of Plate.		Price.	

BILLINGSGATE MARKET

9 An excellent print showing the buildings, river, and fishing-boats. Here Rowlandson is humorous at the expense of the Billingsgate women and their "renowned school of British oratory" £3 3 0

BRITISH MUSEUM

10 View of the Grand Staircase and the Hall of the original Montagu House 2 2 0

BROOKS'S CLUB, ST. JAMES'S STREET

11 An interior of the Great Subscription Room, showing members at play at the tables. This is, of course, the gaming-house built in 1777, and most famous in the days of Fox and the Prince Regent 3 3 0

CARLTON HOUSE

12 The Hall. A fine study in the Classic style of architecture of the Regency 2 2 0

CHAPEL

13 Interior of the Roman Catholic Chapel in Lincoln's Inn Fields 1 10 0

CHELSEA HOSPITAL

14 A most interesting print of the interior of the Great Hall with the scarlet-coated Pensioners seated at dining-tables 2 2 0

CHELSEA, MILITARY COLLEGE

15 Interior showing the cadets receiving instruction 1 10 0

Title of Plate.	Price.

Covent Garden Theatre

31 Interior during choral performance — £1 10 0

Custom House

32 A fine view including the River Thames with an interesting variety of craft afloat and on the foreshore. Tower of London in the distance — 3 3 0

Custom House

33 A fine view of the interior of the Long Room. The Rowlandson figures in this plate are larger and more amusing than usual, embracing a motley crowd of different nationalities — 3 3 0

Debating Society

34 An interior during a meeting held at 22 Piccadilly. The Society was intended to be a nursery of eloquence and preferred to be known as the Athenian Lyceum — 2 2 0

Doctors' Commons

35 An excellent interior view during one of the Courts — 3 3 0

Drury Lane Theatre

36 The interior during a performance — 10 0

Excise Office, Broad Street

37 An unusually fine print of the interior, with some groups of Rowlandson figures in the foreground — 3 3 0

	TITLE OF PLATE.	PRICE.

EXHIBITION OF WATER-COLOURED DRAWINGS, OLD BOND STREET

38 An interior during an Exhibition. The Rowlandson figures are few, but drawn with great care   £2   2   0

FIRE IN LONDON

39 This print is intended to represent the dreadful fire which took place on March 3, 1791, at the Albion Mills, on the Surrey side of Blackfriars Bridge. Fine view of the bridge, the buildings on the opposite side of the river, and St. Paul's in the background. At least five manual fire-engines are engaged on the building and two more are crossing Blackfriars Bridge   2   2   0

FLEET PRISON

40 An unusually fine aquatint with prisoners at play in the yard. This is the prison made famous by Charles Dickens in *Pickwick*   2   2   0

FOUNDLING HOSPITAL

41 Interior of the Chapel during a Service   : 10   0

FREE-MASONS' HALL, GREAT QUEEN STREET

42 A fine plate of the Hall of the Grand Lodge during a banquet and at the time when the female children who are supported by the Society move in procession through the Hall   2   2   0

GREENWICH HOSPITAL

43 Interior of the painted Hall   : 10   0

14

15

MOUNTING GUARD, ST. JAMES'S PARK

No. 60

B

19

TITLE OF PLATE.		PRICE.	

SURREY INSTITUTION

87 Interior during a lecture to a mixed assembly — £1 10 0

SYNAGOGUE, DUKES PLACE, HOUNDSDITCH

88 Interior of the Synagogue belonging to the German Jews. A fine building of the Ionic order built in 1788–90, the cost being defrayed by voluntary contributions, particularly assisted by the generosity of Mrs. Judy Levy, daughter of Moses Hart — 1 10 0

TATTERSALL'S HORSE REPOSITORY

89 An excellent plate representing the Repository during a Sale — 3 3 0

TEMPLE CHURCH

90 Interior of this fine circular 12th-century Church — 2 2 0

TOWER OF LONDON

91 A comprehensive view of the Tower from the outside — 3 3 0

TOWER OF LONDON

92 Interior of the Horse Armoury — 1 10 0

TRADE, BOARD OF

93 Interior of the fine room with figures in consultation around a large table — 2 2 0

TRINITY HOUSE

94 A fine interior with figures — 2 12 6

	TITLE OF PLATE.	PRICE.

VAUXHALL GARDEN

   95 An attractive print of this famous 18th-century pleasure garden, with the illuminated bandstand occupying a prominent position. The figures are very varied and attractive   £2 2 0

WALBROOK

   96 Interior of St. Stephen's Church during a Service   10 0

WATCH HOUSE

   97 Interior of the Watch House, St. Mary le Bone, at night, with the watchmen preparing their lanterns before going on duty. A fine aquatint   3 3 0

WEST INDIA DOCKS

   98 With a fleet of wooden ships at anchor   3 3 0

WESTMINSTER ABBEY

   99 A fine interior view   2 2 0

WESTMINSTER HALL

   100 An interior showing the magnificent wooden ceiling   2 2 0

WHITEHALL

   101 Interior during a Service, with many figures   2 2 0

THE UNIVERSITY OF OXFORD

These, together with the series representing the sister University of Cambridge, are quite unexampled in the history of coloured aquatints. They may indeed be considered the finest work of that extraordinary combination of draughtsmen and engravers who were employed with such success by Rudolph Ackermann at the end of the 18th and beginning of the 19th centuries. It will suffice to state that the drawings are worthy of the splendid architecture they commemorate, and that the aquatint engravings by the masters result in a collection of plates of unequalled merit in their particular line.

The series embraces all the OLD COLLEGE BUILDINGS and GARDENS, with some excellent general views of the CITY OF OXFORD, together with the COSTUMES of MEMBERS of the UNIVERSITY.

The plates measure 10¾ in. x 8 in., printed surface, with good margins beyond this, giving a total measurement of 13⅜ x 11 inches.

A few plates are half-size and measure 5 in. x 7½ in. They are all fine impressions, and were published in 1814.

COLLEGES AND HALLS

ALBAN HALL

105	Now Merton College, with fine view of Merton Street	F. Mackenzie	J. Hill	£2 2	0

ALL SOULS

106	As seen from the top of Radcliffe Library	A. Pugin	J. Bluck	2 2	0
107	The Library, interior (See also under T. Malton)	„	„	1	0
108	Chapel, interior	F. Mackenzie	J. C. Stadler	1 1	0

BALLIOL COLLEGE

109	The Quadrangle	F. Mackenzie	J. Bluck	2 2	0

BRAZEN-NOSE COLLEGE

110	From the quadrangle, showing the gallery and dome of the Radcliffe Library	A. Pugin	J. Bluck	2 2	0
111	The College, part of the Schools, etc., taken from the top of Radcliffe Library	F. Mackenzie	J. Hill	2 2	0

TITLE OF PLATE.	ARTIST.	ENGRAVER.	PRICE.

CHRIST CHURCH

112	The Library and part of Peckwater Quad.	F. Mackenzie	F. C. Lewis	£2 2 0
113	The Library, interior	,,	J. C. Stadler	1 1 0
114	The Cathedral, interior	W. Westall	W. Bennett	2 2 0
115	Do. the Choir	F. Nash	F. C. Lewis	1 10 0
116	Do. (An exterior view will be found described under Corpus Christi College)			
117	The Staircase, small-size plate	A. Pugin	D. Howell	0 15 0
118	Chapter House, interior	F. Mackenzie	J. Bluck	1 10 0
119	The Kitchen, a very animated scene at the enormous grill	A. Pugin	F. C. Lewis	1 10 0
120	The Hall, fine interior	A. Pugin	J. Bluck	1 10 0
121	Tom Gate and Tower. Fine view, with part of Pembroke College and St. Aldate's Church	F. Mackenzie	J. Reeves	2 2 0

CORPUS CHRISTI COLLEGE

| 122 | From the Garden, showing Christ Church Cathedral adjoining and Tom Tower in the distance | W. Westall | J. C. Stadler | 2 2 0 |

Title of Plate.	Artist.	Engraver.	Price.
Exeter College			
123 A view of the Library from the garden, and the Public Schools	F. Nash	J. Hill	£2 2 0
124 The Hall, interior	A. Pugin	J. Bluck	1 10 0
Hertford College			
125 A view from the garden, small-size plate	W. Westall	J. C. Stadler	0 15 0
Jesus College			
126 The Chapel, interior	W. Westall	W. Bennett	1 1 0
Lincoln College			
127 The Chapel, interior from the Ante-Chapel	F. Mackenzie	G. Lewis	1 1 0
Magdalen College			
128 The Old Gate	A. Pugin	J. Bluck	1 10 0
129 The Cloister, with figures on the Lawn	A. Pugin	J. Bluck	1 10 0
130 West Entrance to the Chapel	F. Mackenzie	D. Havell	1 1 0
131 The Chapel, interior	A. Pugin	G. Lewis	1 1 0
132 The Entrance Gate, small-size plate	A. Pugin	D. Havell	0 15 0
133 The Tower and Bridge, with pleasant view of the Cherwell	F. Nash	G. Lewis	3 3 0
(See also under T. Malton)			

Title of Plate.	Artist.	Engraver.	Price.
Magdalen Hall			
134 Exterior, with entrance gate, small-size plate	F. Mackenzie	J. Bluck	£0 15 0
Merton College			
135 The Chapel, interior	A. Pugin	J. Bluck	1 1 0
136 North Window of the Ante-Chapel (See also Alban Hall (above), and Magpie Lane (under General Views).)	A. Pugin	J. Sutherland	1 10 0
New Inn Hall			
137 From the garden	F. Mackenzie	J. Bluck	0 15 0
New College			
138 The Entrance Gate in New College Lane, small-size plate	A. Pugin	J. Hill	0 15 0
139 The Sir Joshua Reynold's Window, painted from his designs on the glass by Jervas		G. Lewis	1 1 0
140 The Chapel, interior	F. Mackenzie	J. C. Stadler	1 1 0
Oriel College			
141 The College, from the quadrangle, with the top of Merton Tower in the background	F. Nash	F. C. Lewis	2 2 0

Title of Plate.	Artist.	Engraver.	Price.
Pembroke College			
142 An attractive small-size plate of this College, famous for its many literary men, including: William Camden, Sir Thomas Browne, Sir Wm. Blackstone, Shenstone, Dr. Samuel Johnson, and William Morris	W. Westall	J. C. Stadler	£0 15 0
Queen's College			
143 Fine view of High Street, showing front of the College	A. Pugin	J. Hill	2 2 0
144 The Chapel, interior	,,	J. C. Stadler	1 1 0
St. Edmund's Hall			
145 A pretty view from the garden, small-size plate	A. Pugin	J. Hill	0 15 0
St. John's College			
146 View the College from the garden of	F. Mackenzie	J. Hill	1 10 0
147 The famous Archbishop Laud quadrangle designed by Inigo Jones	A. Pugin	,,	2 2 0

28

TITLE OF PLATE.	ARTIST.	ENGRAVER.	PRICE.

ST. MARY'S HALL

148 View from the garden, small-size plate } A. Pugin — F. C. Lewis — £0 10 6

TRINITY COLLEGE

| 149 | Fine view of the Chapel | A. Pugin | J. Bluck | 2 2 0 |
| 150 | The Interior of the Library | " | D. Havell | 1 1 0 |

UNIVERSITY COLLEGE

151 Fine view of High Street, showing front of the College } A. Pugin — J. Hill — 2 2 0

152 An interior view of the Hall — " — " — : 10 0

WADHAM COLLEGE

153 A fine general view, showing the front of Wadham and the east end of Broad Street } A. Pugin — J. Hill — 3 3 0

154 The Chapel, interior with the fine screen in the foreground } F. Mackenzie — J. Bluck — 1 1 0

WORCESTER COLLEGE

155 A view from the lawn — W. Westall — J. Stadler — 1 10 0

GENERAL VIEWS

156 View of Oxford taken from New College Tower } W. Westall — J. Bluck — 2 2 0

GENERAL VIEWS (*continued*)

	Title of Plate	Artist	Engraver	Price
157	High Street looking west. This fine view embraces University College, Queen's College, St. Mary's Church, and the City Church in the distance	A. Pugin	J. Bluck	£3 3 0
158	Entrance to Oxford from the London Road. Undoubtedly the finest plate in this collection. It shows in the foreground Magdalen Bridge and Tower, and in the distance the Towers of the City rise above the trees on the banks of the Cherwell	F. Nash	F. C. Lewis	3 13 6
159	The Old Tower. This is the famous Tower adjoining the 11th-century Castle from which the Empress Maud made her romantic escape in the snow in 1142	A. Pugin	J. Bluck	2 2 0
160	St. Aldate's from Carfax. A fine view showing Carfax Church, the Town Hall, and other buildings long since demolished. In the distance is Christ Church with Tom Tower	A. Pugin	J. Hill	3 3 0

	TITLE OF PLATE.	ARTIST.	ENGRAVER.	PRICE.

GENERAL VIEWS (*continued*)

	TITLE OF PLATE.	ARTIST.	ENGRAVER.	PRICE.
161	Magpie Lane (now Grove Street). A busy scene, with more figures than usual. Merton Chapel Tower and entrance to Christ Church meadows in background	A. Pugin	J. Bluck	£3 3 0
162	Bodleian Library, interior	„	J. C. Stadler	1 1 0
163	Radcliffe Library	F. Mackenzie	J. Bluck	1 10 0
164	„ interior	„	„	0 10 6
165	„ vestibule	„	J. Hill	0 10 6
166	View of Oxford, from the Gallery in the Observatory	W. Turner	J. Bluck	2 2 0
167	St. Peter's Church, exterior	A. Pugin	R. Reeve	1 1 0
168	„ the Crypt	F. Nash	J. Bluck	0 10 6
169	St. Mary's Church, taken from the top of Radcliffe Library	F. Nash	F. C. Lewis	2 2 0
170	The Statue Gallery	W. Westall	„	0 10 6
171	Astronomical Observatory. Fine view from the grounds	„	J. C. Stadler	1 1 0
172	Astronomical Observatory. Interior and instruments	F. Mackenzie	J. Bluck	0 10 6
173	Porch of St. Mary's Church, small-size plate	A. Pugin	D. Havell	0 15 0

31

TITLE OF PLATE.	ARTIST.	ENGRAVER.	PRICE.
GENERAL VIEWS (*continued*)			
174 Botanic Garden, the Wren Gateway, small-size plate	A. Pugin	D. Havell	£0 15 0
175 Door of the Divinity School	,,	,,	0 10 6
176 Divinity School, interior	F. Mackenzie	F. C. Lewis	1 1 0
177 Clarendon Printing House, Sheldonian Theatre, and Museum, a fine view of the east end of Broad Street	,,	J. C. Stadler	2 2 0
COSTUMES. All 10s. each.			
178 Vice-Chancellor; Esquire Beadle, Verger, Yeoman Beadle	T. Unwins	J. Agar	
179 Servitor; Bachelor of Divinity; Collector	,,	,,	
180 Gentleman Commoner and Nobleman, undress gowns; Pro Proctor	,,	,,	
181 Proctor	,,	,,	
182 Scholar	,,	,,	
183 Student in Civil Law	,,	,,	
184 Commoner	,,	,,	
185 Nobleman	,,	,,	
186 Bachelor of Arts	,,	,,	
187 Master of Arts	,,	,,	

TITLE OF PLATE.	ARTIST.	ENGRAVER.
COSTUMES (*continued*)		
188 Doctor of Music	T. Unwins	J. Agar
189 Bachelor of Laws	,,	,,
190 Doctor in Physic	,,	,,
191 ,, full dress	,,	,,
192 Doctor in Divinity, in Convocation	,,	,,
193 ,, ,,	,,	,,

These Costume Plates are a combination of etching and stipple, most delicately tinted. The beauty of the features is a noticeable charm.

Also the following fine aquatints by T. MALTON, published in 1802. **30s. each.**

194 Entrance to All Souls College, and St. Mary's Church, from the High Street. Published Feb. 24, 1802

195 The Clarendon Printing House, and view of Broad Street. Published Dec. 31, 1802

196 The First Quadrangle of Magdalen College. Published Dec. 31, 1802

THE UNIVERSITY OF CAMBRIDGE

A series of brilliant coloured aquatints, embracing all the FINE OLD COLLEGE BUILDINGS, exteriors and interiors, a few attractive GENERAL VIEWS, and the COSTUMES peculiar to members of the University.

These prints are most successful in reproducing all the beauty and charm associated with this renowned seat of learning.

The plates measure 10⅝ in. × 8 in., printed surface, with ample margins in addition, making a total area of approximately 13½ in. × 10¾ in.

They are guaranteed to be fine original impressions published in 1815.

	Title of Plate.	Artist.	Engraver.	Price.

COLLEGES AND HALLS

Bene't College

199 The Chapel	W. Westall	D. Havell	£1 10 0

Caius College

200 The College	A. Pugin	D. Havell	3 3 0
201 The Chapel	F. Mackenzie	J. Stadler	1 5 0

Catharine Hall

202 The Chapel	F. Mackenzie	J. Bluck	1 10 0

Christ College

203 The College, from the street	W. Westall	J. Bluck	3 3 0
204 The Chapel	A. Pugin	J. C. Stadler	1 10 0

Clare Hall

205 Clare Hall, showing the Cam and bridge	A. Pugin	J. Bluck	3 3 0
206 The Chapel	F. Mackenzie	J. Stadler	1 5 0
207 Entrance to the Avenue from Clare Hall Piece	W. Westall	,,	3 3 0

Downing College

208 The College. A fine extensive view	W. Westall	D. Havell	2 2 0

ST JOHN'S COLLEGE, CAMBRIDGE, FROM THE GARDENS

NO 234

Title of Plate.	Artist.	Engraver.	Price.

EMMANUEL COLLEGE

209 The College. Fine view of quadrangle with lawn	F. Mackenzie	J. C. Stadler	£3 3 0
210 The College, from the street	A. Pugin	J. Stadler	3 3 0
211 The Chapel	,,	J. C. Stadler	1 10 0
212 The Hall	,,	J. Bluck	1 10 0

JESUS COLLEGE

213 The College, from the Close	W. Westall	J. Stadler	3 3 0
214 The Ante-Chapel	F. Mackenzie	J. Bluck	1 10 0

KING'S COLLEGE

215 Plan and Section of the Roof	F. Mackenzie	J. Bluck	0 10 0
216 Interior of the Chapel	A. Pugin	J. C. Stadler	2 2 0
217 Choir of the Chapel	F. Mackenzie	,,	⸱ 10 0
218 West Porch to Chapel	,,	,,	1 10 0
219 South Porch to Chapel	A. Pugin	J. Bluck	1 10 0
220 The Chapel, the south side and lawn	F. Mackenzie	D. Havell	2 2 0
221 West End to Chapel, and lawn	,,	,,	2 2 0
222 The Court of the College		,,	2 2 0

Title of Plate.	Artist.	Engraver.	Price.
MAGDALENE COLLEGE			
223 The Chapel	F. Mackenzie	J. Bluck	£1 10 0
224 The Library, exterior view with lawn	W. Westall	J. Stadler	2 2 0
PEMBROKE HALL			
225 The College, from a window at Peter-House	F. Mackenzie	J. C. Stadler	3 3 0
226 The Hall or College. An attractive street scene	A. Pugin	J. Stadler	3 3 0
QUEENS' COLLEGE			
227 The College, with river and wooden bridge	W. Westall	J. C. Stadler	3 3 0
228 The College, from the Garden Walks	„	J. Bluck	3 3 0
229 The Hall	A. Pugin	„	1 10 0
ST. JOHN'S COLLEGE			
230 The Second Court	W. Westall	J. C. Stadler	3 3 0
231 The College, from Fisher's Lane. Fine river view	„	„	3 3 0
232 The Chapel	F. Mackenzie	„	1 10 0
233 The Library	W. Westall	D. Havell	1 10 0
234 The College, from the Gardens	F. Mackenzie	R. Reeve	3 3 0

Title of Plate.	Artist.	Engraver.	Price.
St. Peter's College			
235 Part of the College, from private garden	W. Westall	J. Stadler	£2 2 0
236 The Court	F. Mackenzie	J. C. Stadler	2 2 0
237 The Chapel	A. Pugin	D. Havell	1 5 0
238 The College	,,	J. C. Stadler	3 3 0
Sidney College			
239 The Hall. Charming interior	A. Pugin	D. Havell	2 2 0
Trinity College			
240 The Gate	W. Westall	J. Stadler	2 2 0
241 The Hall	A. Pugin	J. Bluck	1 10 0
242 The Quadrangle, with fountain	W. Westall	,,	3 3 0
243 The Chapel	F. Mackenzie	,,	1 10 0
244 The Kitchen	W. H. Pyne	J. C. Stadler	1 10 0
245 The Library, interior	A. Pugin	D. Havell	1 10 0
246 The Library, exterior. Fine elevation and river view	W. Westall	J. Stadler	2 2 0
247 Trinity College Bridge. Fine river view	,,	,,	3 3 0
248 The Colonnade under Trinity Library	,,	,,	1 10 0

TITLE OF PLATE.	ARTIST.	ENGRAVER.	PRICE.
TRINITY HALL			
249 The Front	A. Pugin	J. C. Stadler	£3 3 0
GENERAL VIEWS			
250 View of Cambridge from the Ely Road	W. Westall	J. C. Stadler	2 12 6
251 Law School	F. Mackenzie	,,	1 10 0
252 Theatre of Anatomy	A. Pugin	,,	1 0 0
253 Exterior of Public Library and Senate House	F. Mackenzie	J. Stadler	2 2 0
254 Interior of Public Library and Senate House	,,	D. Havell	1 10
255 Senate House, interior	A. Pugin	,,	10
256 St. Mary's Church, exterior	,,	,,	2 0
257 ,, interior	W. Westall	J. Stadler	1 10
258 Botanic Garden	,,	,,	1 10
259 St Sepulchre's Church, exterior	A. Pugin	J. Hill	1 10
260 ,, ,, interior	,,	,,	1 0
261 Trinity Church	,,	D. Havell	2 2 8
262 Prison and Castle, from the Huntingdon Road	W. Westall	J. C. Stadler	2 2 0

COLOURED AQUATINTS OF THE RIVER THAMES

COMPRISING PLACES OF INTEREST FROM ITS SOURCE TO THE SEA

These charming prints are from a series of drawings made by Joseph Farington, R.A., and are engraved by J. C. Stadler.

Note.—Joseph Farington, R.A., has of late become famous through the discovery and publication of his Diary.

Except in the few cases indicated the price is 25s. per print.

Unless otherwise stated the plates measure 12¾ in. × 8½ in., printed surface, with ample margins in addition.

Dunrobin Castle, Sutherlandshire

DUNROBIN CASTLE, SUTHERLANDSHIRE

NO. 601

		£	s	d
301	Greenwich and up the River	£1	5	0
302	„ and down the River	1	5	0
303	„ from Deptford Yard		5	0
304	Hampton Court		5	0
305	Hardwick and Maple Durham	-	5	0
306	Henley	1	5	0
307	Kemble, Bridge in Meadow	1	5	0
308	Lambeth, View from Millbank	2	2	0
309	Langley Ware	1	5	0
310	Lechlade, Junction of Thames and Canal	:	5	0
311	London—View of Black Fryers Bridge from Sommerset Place	2	2	0
312	„ Battersea, Chelsea and London from Mr. Rucker's Villa	2	2	0
313	„ London Bridge	2	2	0
314	„ The Tower	1	5	0
315	„ View from Lambeth. Large plate measuring 21¾ in. x 13 in.	3	10	0
316	„ View from Greenwich Park. Large plate	3	10	0
317	„ View of Somerset Place and the Adelphi, from Temple Garden	2	2	0
318	„ View up the River from Milbank	1	5	0
319	Maidenhead, Hensor Lodge	:	5	0
320	Maidstone	1	5	0
321	Nuneham, View from the Woods	.	5	0

322	Nuneham, View towards Oxford	£1	5	0
323	Oxford, View in Broad Street	1	5	0
324	,,	1	5	0
325	,, View of High Street	1	5	0
326	Pangborn and Whitchurch from Purley	1	5	0
327	Park Place, Scene at, including Druid's Temple	1	5	0
328	Penshurst	1	5	0
329	Pope's House	1	5	0
330	Putney Bridge	1	5	0
331	Reading, View from Caversham	1	5	0
332	Richmond Hill, from up the River	1	10	0
333	,, from down the River	1	10	0
334	,, from Twickenham	1	10	0
335	Richmond, with Bridge	1	10	0
336	Rochester Bridge, and Castle	1	5	0
337	Rochester and Chatham. Large plate 21 in. × 13 in.	3	10	0
338	Sion House, View from Kew Garden	1	5	0
339	Stanton Harcourt	1	5	0
340	Strawberry Hill	1	5	0
341	Streatley and Goring	1	5	0
342	Temple and Harleford	1	5	0
343	Thames Head	1	5	0
344	Tunbridge Castle	1	5	0

THE FINE COLOURED AQUATINTS

OF THE COAST TOWNS AND SCENERY OF ENGLAND, SCOTLAND AND WALES, BY WILLIAM DANIELL, R.A.

[1769–1837]

These beautiful prints are the outcome of a voyage made partly by sea and partly by land over a period of ten years from 1814 to 1824.

The artist started from Land's End and, continuing by the north coast of Cornwall, proceeded along the coast of Wales, of Scotland, the east and south coasts of England, ending his itinerary at Land's End. He illustrated every town and place of interest in a succession of prints unsurpassed in delicacy of drawing and tinting.

The following is a complete list of these prints arranged alphabetically under Counties for convenience of reference.

The prints measure 9¼ in. × 6¼ in., printed surface, and have good margins. They are guaranteed to be genuine old impressions published in the years 1814 to 1825.

We have copies of the plates on both thick and thin paper, and we offer them at

£2 : 2s. each, on thick paper
30s. each, on thin paper

A brief account of William Daniell will be found on p. 59.

CHESHIRE

354 Hoyle Lake, View near

CORNWALL

355 Boscastle Pier
356 East Looe from Trenant
357 Fowey, from Bodenick
358 Fowey Castle
359 Falmouth
360 Gorranhaven
361 Lizard Lighthouses
362 Land's End (two views)
363 Longships Lighthouse
364 Mevagissy, In the Harbour
365 Mevagissy, Entrance to the Harbour
366 Mullyan
367 Mullyan, near
368 Penzance
369 Polkerris
370 Portlooe
371 Port Reath, Entrance to
372 Portwrinkle
373 Polperro

CORNWALL—*continued*

374 St. Michael's Mount
375 St. Michael's Mount, distant view

CUMBERLAND

376 Harrington, near Whitehaven
377 Maryport
378 Whitehaven

DEVONSHIRE

379 Babicombe
380 Bovisand, near Plymouth
381 Brixham, Torbay
382 Catwater, Plymouth
383 Clovelly
384 Comb Martin, View near
385 Dartmouth, The Junction of the Dart and the Sea
386 Dartmouth, The Entrance
387 Exmouth
388 Hamoaze, Plymouth
389 Hartland Pier
390 Ilfracombe
391 Ilfracombe from Hillsborough

£2 : 2s. each, on thick paper.   30s. each, on thin paper

£2 : 2s. each, on thick paper. 30s. each, on thin paper

KENT

429 Broadstairs
430 Deal Castle
431 Dover Castle
432 Dover, from Shakespeare Cliff
433 Dungeness Lighthouse
434 Folkestone
435 Hythe
436 Margate
437 North Foreland Lighthouse
438 Ramsgate
439 Reculvers
440 Shakespeare Cliff
441 Sheerness
442 Walmer Castle

LANCASHIRE

443 Lancaster Castle
444 Liverpool from Cheshire
445 Liverpool, Seacomb Ferry
446 Liverpool, Townsend Mill
447 Lower Heysham
448 Peel Castle

LINCOLNSHIRE

449 Boston

NORFOLK

450 Yarmouth

NORTHUMBERLAND

451 Bamborough Castle
452 Berwick-upon-Tweed
453 North Shields
454 Tynemouth

SCOTLAND—ABERDEENSHIRE

455 Aberdeen
456 Bridge of Don
457 Fraserburgh
458 Kinnard Head Lighthouse
459 Peterhead
460 Slanes Castle

ARGYLESHIRE

461 Ardnamurchan
462 Dunstaffnage Castle
463 Dunolly Castle
464 Duntrune Castle

£2 : 2s. each, on thick paper.   30s. each, on thin paper

ARGYLESHIRE—*continued*

465 Inverary Castle
466 Loch Swene
467 Miongarry Castle
468 Mount Stuart
469 Rassella

ARRAN ISLAND

470 Loch Ranza

AYRSHIRE

471 Ardrossan, from near
472   „   Pier at
473 Ayr
474 Crag of Ailsa
475 Culzeam Castle

BANFFSHIRE

476 Banff
477 Boyne Castle
478 Duff House
479 Finlater Castle

CAITHNESS-SHIRE

480 Ackergill Tower
481 Berrydale

CAITHNESS-SHIRE—*continued*

482 Berrydale, Castle of
483 Dunbeath Castle
484 Duncansby Stacks
485 Forze Castle
486 Hempriggs, A Scene at
487 Hempriggs, The Stack of
488 Holburn, Clett Rock
489 John o' Groats
490 Keiss Castle
491 Mey Castle
492 Sinclair and Girnigo Castles
493 Skarskerry
494 Thurso
495   „   Castle Sinclair
496   „   Castle Hill
497 Wick
498 Wick, Old Castle

DUMBARTONSHIRE

499 Steamboat on the Clyde near Dumbarton

DUMFRIESSHIRE

500 Caertaveroc Castle

£2 : 2s. each, on thick paper. 30s. each, on thin paper

EDINBURGH
- 501 Edinburgh, distant view
- 502   „   from the Calton Hill
- 503   „   from the Castle
- 504   „   with part of the N. Bridge
- 505 Leith

EIGG ISLAND
- 506 Scor Eigg

ELGINSHIRE
- 507 Brugh Head
- 508 Caxton Tower, near Elgin
- 509 Nelson's Tower, Forres
- 510 Obelisk at Forres

FIFE
- 511 St. Andrews
- 512 Wemyss Castle

FORFARSHIRE
- 513 Broughty Castle
- 514 Dundee
- 515 Montrose

HADDINGTONSHIRE
- 516 Bass Rock
- 517 Dunbar
- 518 Tantallon Castle

HARRIS ISLAND
- 519 Rowardill
- 520 Lighthouse on the Isle of Scalpa

HOLY ISLAND
- 521 View of

HOY ISLAND
- 522 Berryhead
- 523 Old Man of Hoy
- 524 Snook

INVERNESS-SHIRE
- 525 Bay of Barrisdale, Loch Hourne
- 526 Glencoe, from near Ballachulish
- 527 Ilan Dreoch
- 528 Inverness
- 529 Loch of Hourne Head

JURA ISLAND
- 530 View of

£2 : 2s. each, on thick paper. 30s. each, on thin paper

£2: 2s. each, on thick paper. 30s. each, on thin paper

£2 : 2s. each, on thick paper. 30s. each, on thin paper

SUTHERLANDSHIRE—*continued*
- 598 Cuniag, Loch Inver
- 599 Helmsdale
- 600 Dornoch
- 601 Dunrobin Castle
- 602   „   from the N.E.
- 603 Rispand, Durness
- 604 Smowe, Cave of
- 605 Strathnaver
- 606 Tongue, Bay of

SUTHERLANDSHIRE—*continued*
- 607 Unapool, Assynt
- 608 Whitehead, Loch Eribol

WIGTOWNSHIRE
- 609 Dunsky Castle
- 610 Carsleith, near, Galloway
- 611 Mull of Galloway
- 612 Portpatrick
- 613 Wigton

SUFFOLK
- 614 Lowestoft
- 615 Orfordness Lighthouses
- 616 Southwold

SUSSEX
- 617 Arundel
- 618 Beachy Head
- 619 Bovrington, near Brighton

SUSSEX—*continued*
- 620 Brighton
- 621   „   Regent's Square
- 622 Bognor
- 623 Hastings
- 624   „   Whiterock
- 625 Littlehampton
- 626 Rye
- 627 Shoreham
- 628 Winchelsea

£2 : 2s. each, on thick paper. 30s. each, on thin paper

WALES

629 Aberystwith, A View near
630 Air, Point of, Lighthouse
631 Amlwch Harbour, Entrance to
632 Anglesea, Black Marble Quarry
633 Barmouth, Merionethshire
634 Bangor, Bath built by Lord Penrhyn
635 Beaumaris Castle
636 Britton's Ferry
637 Caernarvon Castle from Anglesea
638 Conway Castle
639 Eligug Stack, near St. Gowan's Head
640 Fishguard, Entrance to
641 Goodwich Pier, near Fishguard
642 Holyhead, Harbour Lighthouse
643   „   Rope Bridge
644   „   South Stack (showing the Lighthouse)
645   „   Part of South Stack

WALES—*continued*

646 Mumbles Lighthouse, Swansea Bay
647 Penmanmawr
648 Puffin Island, near Anglesea
649 Red Wharf Bay
650 St. Donats, Glamorganshire
651 Solva, near St. Davids
652 Tenby, Pembrokeshire
653 Worm's Head, Tenby Bay

WESTMORLAND

654 Castlehead
655 Whitbarrow Scar

YORKSHIRE

656 Flamborough Head
657 Hull
658 Scarborough
659 Whitby
660 Whitby Abbey

£2 : 2s. each, on thick paper.   30s. each, on thin paper

WILLIAM DANIELL, R.A.

(1769–1837)

Landscape painter and engraver, produced several important works, often in collaboration with his uncle, THOMAS DANIELL, R.A. (1749–1840). As a youth of fourteen he accompanied his uncle to India, where he remained for ten years, and there laid the foundation of his fame as a Landscape Painter, and, incidentally, as a traveller, for it was no easy task to explore the " beautiful and interesting between Cape Comorin and Sirinagar " at that time. The drawings made during this voyage were engraved in aquatint and published as *Oriental Scenery—or Views in Hindostan*, with 144 plates, and *A Picturesque Voyage to India by way of China*, with 50 plates. The Daniells returned from India in 1795, and William spent most of his time mastering the fashionable art of aquatinta. Twelve coloured aquatints published in 1812 as *Views of London and the Docks in the Neighbourhood*, met with considerable success. It was about this time that he became restless and conceived the idea of making a voyage round the coast of Great Britain, a feature of the country which he considered had suffered undue neglect. He later made this point clear in his Introduction, which includes the following passage:

59

ND - #0095 - 201125 - C0 - 229/152/4 - PB - 9780266116233 - Gloss Lamination